Nutrition

by Ashley Kuehl

Consultant: Caitlin Krieck, Social Studies Teacher and Instructional Coach, The Lab School of Washington

Minneapolis, Minnesota

Credits
Cover and title page, © Caterina Robustelli/iStock; 3, © irin-k/Shutterstock; 4–5, © Pixel-Shot/Shutterstock; 7, © SolStock/iStock; 9, © Antonina Vlasova/Shutterstock; 10–11, © Rimma Bondarenko/Shutterstock; 13, © Aiselin82/iStock; 14–15, © MDV Edwards/Shutterstock; 17, © Oleksandra Naumenko/Shutterstock; 19, © Julia Sudnitskaya/Shutterstock; 21, © Rob Byron/Shutterstock; 22–23, © Ron and Patty Thomas/Shutterstock; 25, © Jim Lambert/Shutterstock; 27, © CarlosBarquero/Shutterstock.

Bearport Publishing Company Product Development Team
Publisher: Jen Jenson; Director of Product Development: Spencer Brinker; Editorial Director: Allison Juda; Editor: Cole Nelson; Editor: Tiana Tran; Production Editor: Naomi Reich; Art Director: Kim Jones; Designer: Kayla Eggert; Designer: Steve Scheluchin; Production Specialist: Owen Hamlin

Statement on Usage of Generative Artificial Intelligence
Bearport Publishing remains committed to publishing high-quality nonfiction books. Therefore, we restrict the use of generative AI to ensure accuracy of all text and visual components pertaining to a book's subject. See BearportPublishing.com for details.

Library of Congress Cataloging-in-Publication Data is available at www.loc.gov or upon request from the publisher.

ISBN: 979-8-89577-074-0 (hardcover)
ISBN: 979-8-89577-521-9 (paperback)
ISBN: 979-8-89577-191-4 (ebook)

Copyright © 2026 Bearport Publishing Company. All rights reserved. No part of this publication may be reproduced in whole or in part, stored in any retrieval system, or transmitted in any form or by any means, electronic, mechanical, photocopying, recording, or otherwise, without written permission from the publisher. Bearport Publishing is a division of FlutterBee Education Group.

For more information, write to Bearport Publishing, 3500 American Blvd W, Suite 150, Bloomington, MN 55431.

Contents

Fuel Up 4
Energy Breakdown. 6
Body Builders and Power Foods 8
Can't Live Without Them 12
Join the Group. 16
A Little Extra. 18
Label It 20
Easy or Nutritious 22
Taking Care of You 26

Read the Label 28
SilverTips for Success 29
Glossary 30
Read More 31
Learn More Online 31
Index 32
About the Author. 32

Fuel Up

At lunchtime, there are so many choices! Many foods taste good. But there's more to think about than just flavor. Food affects your health.

The things you eat **fuel** your body and brain. What will keep you going all day?

Your **diet** is the kinds of things you eat and drink. A healthy diet needs balance. It includes a mix of many kinds of foods.

Energy Breakdown

All living things need energy to do work. Animals, including humans, get their energy from food. A food's energy is measured in calories. Food with more calories has more energy.

Nutrition (noo-TRISH-uhn) is the process of taking in and using food. This involves breaking down food into its key parts.

> Nutrition is also the name for an area of science. It looks at what is in food and what the body does with it. A person who studies this science is a nutritionist.

Energy from food helps us run, think, and even sleep.

Body Builders and Power Foods

Food has **nutrients** that help the body do things. There are many kinds of nutrients.

One type is protein. Proteins help build many parts of the body. They help mend it, too. Nuts, eggs, beans, and meats all have protein.

Your hair, skin, muscles, **organs**, and bones all use protein. One kind of protein even helps move blood through the body.

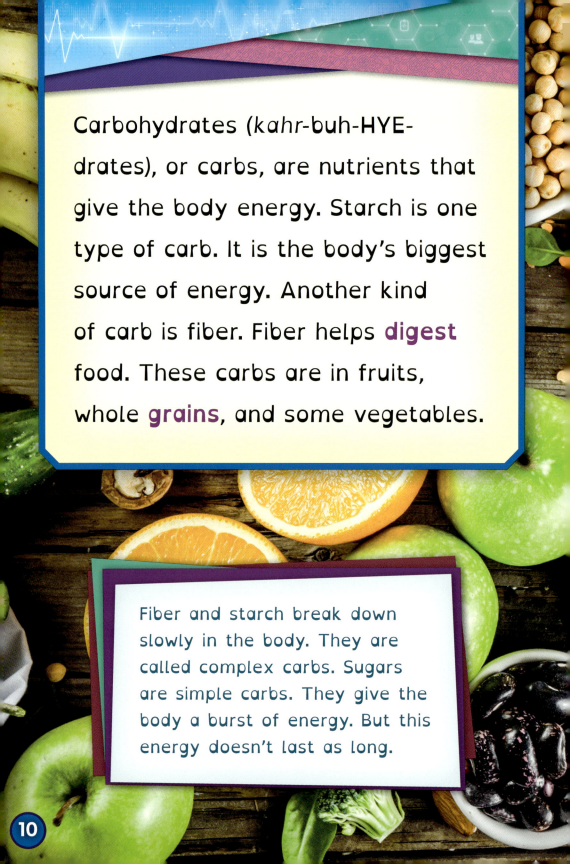

Carbohydrates (kahr-buh-HYE-drates), or carbs, are nutrients that give the body energy. Starch is one type of carb. It is the body's biggest source of energy. Another kind of carb is fiber. Fiber helps **digest** food. These carbs are in fruits, whole **grains**, and some vegetables.

Fiber and starch break down slowly in the body. They are called complex carbs. Sugars are simple carbs. They give the body a burst of energy. But this energy doesn't last as long.

Can't Live Without Them

The body also needs dozens of different vitamins and minerals. These nutrients keep you healthy.

The human body can make some vitamins, but we get most from eating food. Plants **absorb** minerals from water and soil. Humans get minerals from eating plants or animals that eat plants.

> Not having the right vitamins and minerals causes health problems. Without enough vitamin C, a person can get scurvy. This sickness can make people feel tired. It can also make their gums bleed.

Many kinds of fruits and vegetables have vitamins and minerals.

Fats are nutrients that help the body absorb other nutrients. Some fats are better for the body than others. Good fats can give you energy and keep your skin healthy.

Water is the most important nutrient. It keeps the body cool. Water also helps most body systems function.

There are four kinds of fats. Some are needed for long-term health. Others should be avoided. Good fats can be found mainly in vegetables, nuts, seeds, and fish.

Join the Group

Eating many kinds of foods gives a variety of nutrients. Foods are divided into five food groups based on their nutrients. Fruits and vegetables are two main groups. Another one is grains. Protein and dairy make up the last two.

Eating from all the food groups is best. This helps the body get different kinds of nutrients. However, fruits and vegetables should make up about half of a person's diet.

A Little Extra

Foods that are found in nature, such as fruits and vegetables, are called whole foods. They often have many nutrients. However, some foods are made with lots of **ingredients** that are changed from how they are in nature. These are called **processed** foods. They are often less healthy.

> Some foods have **additives**. Additives include salt, sugar, flavorings, and colors. They can change the taste, look, or texture of food. But they often don't help the body.

Processed food with few nutrients is often called junk food.

Label It

How can you know exactly what is in your food? Packaged foods have labels that include this information.

Labels must list every ingredient in the food. They also say how much of certain nutrients are in the food.

Labels have dietary **recommendations**. They say how much of a nutrient there is. This number is often written as a percentage based on the suggested amount needed each day.

Food labels also show the amount of calories in each serving.

Easy or Nutritious

There are a lot of messages about making food choices. Ads tell us to buy certain foods. But many of these ads are for processed foods. They may not have many nutrients.

Sometimes, friends or family share their ideas about food. They may pressure others about what to eat.

> It's normal to think about food and nutrition. However, having frequent worry or fear around food is not healthy. It is important to ask for help if this happens.

Time and money may play a role in making choices about food. Fast food and processed foods are often quick, easy, and cheap. But they can have few vitamins or minerals. Eating these foods once in a while is fine. However, bodies work better with food that has more nutrients.

> Some grocery stores sell healthy food options that are already made. However, they often cost more money than buying the ingredients to make the dish yourself.

Taking Care of You

Making smart nutrition choices is important for the body. A healthy diet has protein and carbs. It includes foods with vitamins, minerals, and healthy fats. It also requires drinking plenty of water.

You only get one body. It's your job to take care of it.

> Nutrition is one part of wellness. Exercise is important, too. Being responsible for your health also means looking after mental health. It includes keeping healthy relationships.

Read the Label

Food labels have a lot of nutrition information. What do they show?

Serving Size
This tells the size of one portion of the food. The other information on the label is based on one serving.

Fat
Fats help the body absorb nutrients. But eating too much can be bad for the body.

Carbohydrates
These nutrients give the body energy.

Nutrition Facts

Serving Size 3 oz. (240mL)
Servings Per Container 2

Amount Per Serving

Calories 250   Calories from Fat 110

	% Daily Value*
Total Fat 12g	18%
Saturated Fat 3g	15%
Trans Fat 3g	
Cholesterol 30mg	10%
Sodium 470mg	20%
Total Carbohydrate 31g	10%
Dietary Fiber 0g	0%
Sugars 5g	
Protein 5g	

Vitamin A	4%
Vitamin C	2%
Calcium	20%
Iron	4%

*Percent Daily Values are based on a 2,000 calorie diet. Your Daily Values may be higher or lower depending on your calorie needs.

		Calories	2,000	2,500
Total Fat		Less than	65g	80g
Sat Fat		Less than	25g	25g
Cholesterol		Less than	300mg	300mg
Sodium		Less than	2,400mg	2,400mg
Total Carbohydrate			300g	375g
Dietary Fiber			25g	30g

% Daily Value
This is the recommended amount of what a person may need in a day.

Protein
Protein helps the body grow and repair itself.

Vitamins and Minerals
People need many kinds of vitamins and minerals to stay healthy.

SilverTips for SUCCESS

★ SilverTips for REVIEW

Review what you've learned. Use the text to help you.

Define key terms

carbohydrates protein
fats vitamins
minerals

Check for understanding

Pick two nutrients and explain what they do for the human body.

What are processed foods, and how are they different from whole foods?

What can be found on nutrition labels?

Think deeper

How does nutrition fit into your life? In what ways might you improve your nutrition?

★ SilverTips on TEST-TAKING

- **Make a study plan.** Ask your teacher what the test is going to cover. Then, set aside time to study a little bit every day.

- **Read all the questions carefully.** Be sure you know what is being asked.

- **Skip any questions** you don't know how to answer right away. Mark them and come back later if you have time.

Glossary

absorb to take in or soak up

additives things added to foods to change their qualities

diet what a person or animal usually eats and drinks

digest to break down food inside the body

fuel to provide energy for work

grains seeds that come from plants and are eaten as food

ingredients the foods that are used to make a meal or dish

nutrients substances needed for healthy living and growth

organs body parts that do particular jobs

processed having been changed in some way

recommendations suggestions

Read More

Faust, D. R. *The Digestive System (Body Systems: Need to Know).* Minneapolis: Bearport Publishing, 2025.

McClure, Leigh. *The Digestive System (Scientific American Investigates the Human Body).* Buffalo, NY: Scientific American Educational Publishing, 2025.

Phillips-Bartlett, Rebecca. *Healthy Diet (Live Well!).* Minneapolis: Bearport Publishing, 2024.

Learn More Online

1. Go to **FactSurfer.com** or scan the QR code below.
2. Enter "**Nutrition**" into the search box.
3. Click on the cover of this book to see a list of websites.

Index

additives 18, 24

carbohydrates 10, 26, 28

colors 18

energy 6–7, 10, 14, 28

fats 14, 26, 28

fiber 10

food groups 16

labels 20–21, 28

minerals 12–13, 24, 26, 28

protein 8, 16, 26, 28

salt 18

starch 10

sugar 10, 18

vitamins 12–13, 24, 26, 28

water 12, 14, 26

About the Author

Ashley Kuehl is an editor and writer specializing in nonfiction for young people. She lives in Minneapolis, MN.